WILD ABOUT
FOOD

Aaron Patterson and Wendy Dickinson

TELEVISION PRODUCTIONS LIMITED

For my wife, Clare, son William – and bump
- and for my late Dad, Bill, who was a huge influence on my career.

First published in 2001 by Kingfisher Television Productions,
Carlton Studios, Lenton Lane, Nottingham NG7 2NA

ISBN 0-9540578-0-5

Supported by The East Midlands Media Initiative - part funded by the European Regional Development Fund.

A CIP catalogue record for this book is available from the British Library.

Photography: Gary Moyes, Stuart Wood and Cliff Kent
Front cover photograph: Gary Moyes
Design and production by Charlie Webster and Nick Withers
Printed in Great Britain by the Bath Press.

This book accompanies the television series Wild about Food
© Carlton Television Limited, made by Kingfisher Television Productions.
Produced and directed by John Dickinson
Executive producers: Tony Francis and Duncan Rycroft

Introduction

Living and working in a county like Rutland and at Hambleton Hall is an inspiration to me. I could be cooking in London – and I have in the past – but I know that I'd lose a vital connection with the food I buy and cook.

It's that connection, that knowledge of where food comes from, that makes me want to get up every morning and come to work. For me, cooking is all about understanding food and being excited by it. I never want to lose that passion.

My father, Bill, inspired me to follow in his footsteps and become a chef and he never lost his passion for the business. He most recently owned a restaurant in Southern Ireland and on the day he died, almost two years ago, he had cooked for a packed house.

But it's not just the cooking, it's the raw ingredients as well. For example, when my friend, ex-miner Barry Thompson, comes into the kitchen with a basket of wild mushrooms, I know they were growing a few hours earlier in the woods around Hambleton. The same goes for partridge, pheasant, hares and the pike and crayfish from nearby waters.

I know exactly where the beef and pork I use in the kitchens go to bed at night – thanks to people like stockbroker turned farmer, Jan McCourt, who arrived on my doorstep one day with a sirloin under his arm and turned me on to his fantastic Dexter beef.

When fish is delivered to Hambleton it's not portioned and vacuum-packed as in so many top restaurants, but almost jumping around with freshness – gorgeous turbot, huge, whole cod and scallops collected by divers off the Isle of Skye. And I can catch the trout myself in Rutland Water.

Of course, it's easy for me to cook this way, because I have all the backing of a professional kitchen. I understand that what happens on a packed Saturday night at Hambleton is nothing like your kitchen at home. But I honestly believe that anyone can have fantastic results in the kitchen if they really care about what they eat.

With a little help from me...

Aaron Patterson

Contents

The Recipes

All recipes serve four people except where indicated

Hambleton Hall

The last twenty years has seen a remarkable transformation in restaurant cooking in Britain. Aaron Patterson has been in the thick of it. Restaurant customers are more sophisticated: chefs are more skilful. Together they have brought our island to the point where we are offering to European cuisine a distinctive contribution at the top level. If you sometimes wonder about the roots of this revolution this tale may be of interest.

In 1979 I stumbled upon a rambling Victorian house in a spectacular position overlooking Rutland Water. I had been scheming for some time to find a business which would enable me to base the family in the country and, if possible, earn a living from a business related to my enthusiasm for food, wine and country living.

Hambleton Hall opened with 11 rooms in July, 1980 and a combination of good luck, hard work and talented staff propelled us to wide recognition and success. Our aim has always been to bring together a warm welcome, faultless service, an elegant but comfortable interior, a wine list that excites wine buffs as well as beginners and cooking that justifies a long detour.

Our first head chef was Nicholas Gill, a 21-year-old of prodigious talent and charm who had spent three years in Paris. His time was divided between three restaurants : Paul Chene, an old fashioned bourgeois family restaurant with one Michelin star; Moulin de Village, one of the first Parisian restaurants practising 'nouvelle cuisine' and the legendary Maxims, which produced classic dishes with the finest and most expensive ingredients.

Nick absorbed a great deal from each of these very different places. Paul Chène worked with economical cuts, offal and braises and had a genius for getting the best from the widest range of raw materials at a sensible price.

Moulin de Village introduced Nick to the novel presentational ideas of nouvelle cuisine and, more importantly, to a fixation with freshness and immediacy of flavours.

Maxims gave him a glimpse into the world of Carème and Escoffier where foie-gras, truffles and woodcocks, turbot, lobsters and scallops were washed down with the finest Champagne, Burgundy and Claret.

Within two years of the opening of Hambleton Hall, Nick had won a Michelin star and recognition as one of a select band of new wave young British chefs who were transforming culinary standards outside London.

Aaron Patterson joined Nick Gill as a 16-year-old kitchen apprentice in 1983 and worked with him for three years in all sections of the kitchen, before setting out to perfect his technique with Raymond Blanc at Le Manoir aux Quat Saisons and elsewhere.

In 1993 Aaron returned as head chef and in his seven years at the helm he has remained true to his culinary roots whilst putting his own stamp on the Hambleton style.

Nowhere has he made more individual impact than in the sourcing of individual local ingredients. With Jan McCourt he has developed supplies of naturally reared beef, lamb and pork using flavoursome, slow growing rare breeds such as Dexter and Longhorn cattle, Badger–Faced sheep and Gloucester Old Spot pigs. He has pushed our gardening team to expand greatly our homegrown supplies of herbs, salads and soft fruits and continues to widen the splendid array of game specialities, which liven up the winter months.

Aaron's cooking style has evolved and matured: although he is one of the best technicians of his generation he now has the restraint and confidence to understand that in great cooking 'less can be more' and simple combinations are often the most memorable.

Restaurant cooking is not a solitary art – in this book and on the screen one gets a glimpse of the personality that enables Aaron to enthuse his 12 fellow artists with the dedication needed to make every plate a masterpiece every day.

Readers of this book can see clearly enough that Aaron's food looks wonderful, but we are all of the opinion that taste is much more important. The recipes in this book will enable you to cook Aaron's dishes yourself; alternatively, don't forget that a warm welcome awaits you on the Rutland Riviera, where the culinary revolution continues every day.

Tim Hart

MENU
BREAKFAST

EGG AND TWO BACON	£1·60
EGG, BACON, TOMATOES	£2·40
EGG, BACON, TOMATOES, BUBBLE/CHIPS	£3·00
EGG, BACON, TOMATOES, MUSHROOMS	£3·00
EGG, CHIPS (BUBBLE) & BEANS	£2·30
1 SAUSAGE, EGG, TOMATOES, CHIPS/BUBBLE	£2·80
LIVER, BACON, BUBBLE/CHIPS	£3·00
2 SCRAMBLED/POACHED EGGS ON TOAST	£2·00
BACON, BUBBLE & BEANS	£2·40
2 FRIED EGGS ON TOAST	£2·00

ANY COMBINATION AVAILABLE

(TRY OUR BUBBLE 'N SQUEAK)

WE ALSO HAVE BLACK PUDDING

Breakfast

SCRAMBLED EGGS IN THEIR SHELLS

SMOKED HADDOCK WITH BUBBLE AND SQUEAK,
THE PERFECT POACHED EGG AND CHIVE SAUCE

BREAKFAST SALAD

Traditionally, animosity has always existed between chefs and waiters.

We're always having a go at them and vice versa. But I have to confess that come breakfast time, even I have some shred of sympathy for the front of house staff.

Guests often judge a hotel from the quality of the breakfast service. It starts their day and it has to be right. Breakfast at Hambleton is ordered like a military campaign. It's all about attention to detail.

Of course, there are times when the last thing you need as a waiter is attention to detail. For example, when a female guest unashamedly greets you in the buff as you deliver the breakfast tray. Believe me, it happens quite a lot. Well, maybe only to the lucky ones.

I wasn't quite as lucky when I was tempted to eat breakfast with Barry for our programme on the subject. And certainly, whoever said 'Breakfast like a king, lunch like a prince and sup like a pauper', had obviously never met Barry Thompson.

Ex-miner Barry, supplier of all things wild to the Hambleton kitchen, lives for much of the time in a caravan, in a field, at the back of the house. I've often been in the kitchen, preparing rabbits, and he'll pop up and say 'give us those livers, son'. Then he's off back to his caravan to

have them for breakfast. He claims they're lovely but I can't see it myself. The livers from French farmed rabbits aren't too bad but the livers from wild rabbits are absolutely vile. Anyway, Barry was determined to convert me so I'm invited to the caravan. All I can smell are boiled livers. Horrible. I ate them, but I don't think I'll be going back for seconds.

In his defence, I should say that Barry cooks some great food in his caravan, often gathered and picked wild. I suppose that's one of the reasons I'm so drawn to him. My dad, Bill, who died a couple of years ago, was like Barry. As a kid we'd go salmon fishing on the River Dee and my brother, Andrew, and I would fish for freshwater mussels and look for pearls. Then the three of us would build a camp fire, pick some mushrooms and have breakfast. Barry reminds me of those days.

Having rubbished Barry's livers, I must admit I do love breakfast. Particularly when it's in such a cosmopolitan place as the Borough Café, tucked away in a little side street along the side of the Thames at Southwark.

Jan McCourt, who used to be a bond dealer in the City, has introduced me to two great tastes: the Dexter beef he now rears at his Rutland farm and Mariarenza Moruzzi's bubble and squeak at the Borough Café.

Jan still visits his old City stamping ground every weekend when he sells his beef and pork on the nearby Market. These days, though, the old power breakfasts have given way to Maria's marriage of boiled potatoes and cabbage, which everyone raves about (or at least those in the know do). And, according to Maria, those 'in the know' include Sean Connery, Catherine Zeta Jones and Michael Caine. And now me.

Maria's of Italian descent, of course, as you can tell when the passion builds as she stirs the big vat of bubble and squeak that's been on the go at the café for forty years. Nowadays it's Maria who does all the cooking while her mother (universally referred to by family and regulars alike as 'Mamma') takes the orders and the cash. On camera, Maria tells me that the secret of her bubble and squeak is getting just the right amount of little crispy, charred bits. But when the cameras were turned off Mamma raised a quizzical Napolitan eyebrow.

Let's get the pecking order right, then. Mamma assures me that actually she was responsible for starting the bubble and squeak regime at the Borough Café forty years ago. And long before that it was her mamma's recipe.

"Bubble and squeak in Naples?" I ask. I'm genuinely surprised and tell her so.

Mamma says : "We were poor. Sometimes we had it every day – sometimes twice a day."

Who am I to argue? I have to admit that I had double helpings that day. A bubble and squeak sandwich at the crack of dawn and a bit later, bubble and squeak with egg and bacon.

I thoroughly enjoyed Maria's cooking, obviously because it was so good but also because the atmosphere was right and I was in the mood. That's the thing about breakfast. It's a very personal thing. You're always feeling at your most sensitive in the mornings, mood-wise and taste-wise. Sometimes you don't want anything. But if I'm in the right mood and I sit down with my wife Clare and son, William, I love it.

Another great breakfast memory was at Billingsgate Market in London years ago. It was early. I was hungry. And I was expecting the bog-standard greasy fry-up, but instead they had smoked salmon and scrambled eggs on the menu. They were perfect. Here's my version of that popular dish and my spin on Maria's bubble and squeak. When you get the time, and if you're in the mood, try them.

Presenting scrambled eggs in the shells isn't new but it's a really fun way to start the day. It looks stunning but is very simple. I use the wonderful, free-range eggs from our own hens. This dish also makes a perfect starter.

Scrambled Eggs in their shells

Hold a fresh raw egg firmly on a chopping board and use a small serrated knife to gently score around the pointed end, about 2cm (three-quarters of an inch) from the tip. Increase the pressure until the top of the egg comes away. It's easier than it sounds! Put the raw egg into the bowl. Repeat with the other two eggs. Rinse out the shells and caps and wipe dry.

Whisk the eggs well and scramble gently, whisking all the time, over a medium heat until they start firming up. Remove from the heat when almost done, as the eggs will continue cooking in the warmth of the pan. We don't want sloppy eggs but neither should they be too firm. Don't season the eggs until this stage as seasoning when they're raw discolours the mixture.

Using a teaspoon, fill the empty shells with scrambled eggs. Turn the caps upside down to form a cup shape and place one on top of each egg. Put a spoonful of sour cream into each cap, then top one with caviar, one with smoked salmon and one with either truffle shavings or mushrooms.

Serve with a basket of Warm Brioche Soldiers.

Serves One:

3 fresh eggs

3 tablespoons sour cream

Teaspoon each caviar, chopped smoked salmon and truffle shavings or finely chopped sautéed mushrooms

2 tablespoons butter

Smoked Haddock with bubble and squeak, the perfect poached egg and chive sauce

Mix the beaten eggs into the mashed potatoes then add the cooked cabbage, peas and spinach and mix well. Season. Put four oiled metal ring moulds 8cm x 4cm deep (3in x 1.5in deep) into an oiled, non-stick baking dish and fill with the bubble and squeak mixture, pressing down well. Smooth the tops and bake in the oven at 200°C/400°F/Gas Mark 6 for 5 minutes until the top is just firm. Turn over with a fish slice, run a sharp blade around the edges, remove the moulds and bake for a further 5 minutes until golden. Meanwhile, poach the fish gently in milk for 2 minutes each side. When cooked, keep in a warm place and strain 200ml (7fl oz) of the cooking liquid into a clean pan and whisk in a tablespoon of butter to thicken slightly. Season with salt and pepper and a squeeze of lemon juice and stir in the snipped chives and tomatoes. In a separate pan, wilt the spinach with a knob of butter and a splash of water.

Try my foolproof method for poaching eggs: it works every time. Immerse the whole eggs in boiling water for 20 seconds then crack each into a ramekin before slipping into barely simmering water for three minutes. The dip in boiling water starts setting the albumen in the egg and helps it maintain a perfect shape.

To serve, make a bed of the wilted spinach in the centre of each plate, top with the bubble and squeak fritter, then the haddock and finally the poached egg. Spoon the chive sauce over the egg and around the edges of the plate and garnish with a sprig of chervil.

---

4 x 100g (4oz) pieces of smoked haddock, boned and skinned

Milk to cover

Tablespoon of butter

Lemon juice

Three medium tomatoes, skinned, de-seeded and diced

Fresh snipped chives

2 large cooked potatoes, mashed with a little cream

4 large eggs, beaten

2 heaped tablespoons cooked, shredded cabbage

2 tablespoons cooked peas

2 tablespoons cooked spinach

Salt and pepper

250g (9oz) spinach

Four whole eggs

This makes a wonderful brunch and couldn't be simpler. It has all the elements of a traditional English breakfast – bacon, eggs, black pudding, fried tomatoes and fried bread – but in a healthier and more interesting combination.

Breakfast Salad

Either fry or bake the baguette slices until crisp in a little olive oil. Grill the bacon until crisp. Boil the eggs for 3.5 minutes, cool in iced water, peel and halve. Pan fry the black pudding in a little olive oil until crisp. Heat a tablespoon of olive oil and cook the tomatoes until they are starting to soften but are still whole. Stir in the shredded basil leaves and I tablespoon of balsamic vinegar.

Dress the salad leaves with the vinaigrette and place a mound in the centre of each plate. Sit the eggs on the croutons around the edge of the leaves (eggs on toast!) and arrange the other ingredients attractively, drizzling over a little extra dressing.

12 thin rashers of
smoked streaky bacon

12 quail eggs

12 slices of black pudding

12 slices from a thin baguette

12 cherry tomatoes

4 basil leaves, shredded

2 tablespoons olive oil

1 tablespoon balsamic vinegar

For the vinaigrette:

4 tablespoons balsamic vinegar

2 tablespoons olive oil

1 teaspoon grain mustard

1 tablespoon water

Mixed salad leaves

Fish
Seasick in Scotland and
50 years of 'Frying Tonight'

COD TEMPURA

SCALLOPS BAKED IN THEIR SHELLS

CRAB COCKTAIL WITH AVOCADO,
TOMATO TARTARE AND GRAPEFRUIT DRESSING

It was the morning after the night before. Except the night before had only ended about three hours ago and now here I am in a thirty-foot boat in rolling seas off the Isle of Seil on the West coast of Scotland.

Scallop diver Andrew Duncan used to be a voice on the end of a telephone to me. I wished I'd kept it that way.

To be fair, Andrew had eaten and drunk even more than me the night before, as Scottish hospitality reached Olympian heights.

My producer, John Dickinson, and I had arrived the night before at about 10 o'clock after a flight from Birmingham to Glasgow and several hours driving, past Loch Lomond, to get to the Isle of Seil. We were shattered and looking forward to a good night's sleep before an early start for a long day's filming. Silly boys.

We discovered that generous-spirited Andrew and his housekeeper, Sue, had prepared a gourmet five-course seafood extravaganza for us (the camera crew had already arrived) to be washed down with various fine wines. Rude to refuse really.

Three hours sleep (well, at least for me. All five of the team slept in the same room and the others complained I'd kept them awake

snoring) and we were up at 6am to be presented with a huge cooked breakfast. The works. Plus a local porridge dish laced with blackberry-flavoured whisky.

After feeding most of the breakfast to the dog, our subterfuge came back to haunt us when the hound threw up in the kitchen. John manfully cleared up the mess and, unable to find a bin, legged it out to the garden and buried the evidence under a bush.

I was feeling truly awful. I must have a strong stomach, though. That morning, as our boat wallowed in heavy seas, I almost followed the dog's example, and threw it clear across Seil Sound.

But we did get some fantastic scallops and Andrew was brilliant. He used to be a stockbroker but now he makes his living diving for scallops, which he's been sending south to me for a quite a few years.

If I hadn't felt quite so ill I'm sure I would have enjoyed the day more, as Andrew put aside his hangover and plumbed the depths for his exceptionally fine-tasting scallops. As it was, I had to force myself to eat a few raw – 'au naturel'- egged on by Andrew and John.

The sad part is that having devoured the raw scallop for posterity, and television, the sea became so rough that a kettle hurtled off the

galley stove, hit the camera and rendered the footage unusable.

I absolutely refused to do a second take.

After our experiences in Scotland the producer tells me we're off to Lincolnshire as David Mellor is taking me fishing for crabs.

The David Mellor? Has he been reduced to donning rubber waders for my gratification?

Of course, common sense prevails, and David Mellor turns out to be 'Dave' Mellor, nursing home assistant and part time crab fisherman on the Lincolnshire coast. Thankfully, this time, it's a landlubbers' sea. Calm as a millpond and in the distance I can still see the funfair at Mablethorpe.

Dave's been fishing these North Sea waters for 20 years and as we haul up the pots he's baited with a few bits of old flounder, I realise what a physical job it is. And you always run the risk of the crab catching you in a pincer movement. Dave's waited as long as two minutes for an enemy crab to release its grip on his hand.

I look on wimpishly and scuttle back to Hambleton to turn the beast into crab cocktail ... but before I do, we stop off in the tiny village of Upton, near Gainsborough, to sample what some people say are the best fish and chips in Britain.

I'm also keen to pick up some tips from 86-year-old Kathleen Longden, who has been frying fish at her shop for over 50 years. Her grandson, John, has to bring in the coal to fire up the ovens for her now, but Kathleen still goes to the market with her buckets to buy the fish. And she makes the batter, and does the frying.

She's a formidable character – a real matriarch, standing behind the immaculate art deco coal-fired range that was originally installed in the Fifties. She's definitely in charge and I can see she's not impressed with me. Which is as it should be. I show her the respect she deserves ... but she still won't part with her secret batter recipe. The charm has failed.

Come frying time and they're queuing around the corner. Kathleen only opens three days a week and people come from far and wide.

I stand outside with scalding hot fish and chips wrapped in yesterday's papers and think that food doesn't get much better than this.

I'll be cooking Cod Tempura back at Hambleton – may Kathleen forgive me.

You may think this sounds so unusual that it can't possibly work but it's sensational. The batter is so light and when the fish fries the carrots and leeks stick out like a punk haircut. It ends up looking a bit like a hedgehog. I don't know what Kathleen would make of it but I really recommend that you try cod cooked this way. I serve the fish with big, fat, square-cut chips, about ten or fifteen for each person. I've worked out a foolproof way of cooking chips because I'm absolutely sick of eating ones that are either too thin, too crispy, undercooked or just simply cold by the time you get them into your mouth. My method gives you chips that stay hot, with a crispy golden outside and a light, fluffy middle.

Cod Tempura

Cut 10 to 15 big chips for each person – at least the thickness of a thumb – and square off the ends. There will be some potato wasted but it's worth it for the final presentation. Blanch the chips in oil heated to 180°C/350°F for 2 minutes then drain, cool and freeze in a single layer on a baking sheet for 2 to 3 hours. Cook from frozen in hot oil until crisp and golden.

For each serving lay out a sheet of cling film 50cm x 25cm (20in x 10in). Sprinkle with the carrots and leeks, place a piece of cod in the middle and sprinkle with more vegetables. Bring the sides of the cling film up towards you so that the cod is enclosed in a lattice of vegetables. It's a bit like wrapping a Christmas pudding in a cloth. Press the vegetables firmly around the fish before twisting the gathered cling film together and tying with a piece of string. Leave to chill in the fridge for at least four hours.

Mix all the dry batter ingredients together and slowly whisk in ice-cold water until you have a thin batter. Don't make this until you are ready to cook.

Heat oil in a pan or deep fat fryer to 180°C/350°F. Carefully remove the fish from the cling film. Some vegetables will fall away but most will stay around the fish. Dunk the ball of fish in the batter, quickly drain off the excess and pop into the hot fat. Cook for 4–5 minutes. The shredded vegetables will spring out of the batter. Serve with two clusters of chips and separate puddles of ketchup, tartare sauce and mushy peas.

4 x 150g (5oz) chunky pieces of skinless and boneless cod

2 carrots, shredded like spaghetti

2 leeks, finely shredded

For the batter:

200g (7oz) plain flour

200g (7oz) cornflour

25g (1oz) baking powder

25g (1oz) salt

iced water

8 large potatoes

Tomato ketchup

Tartare sauce

Mushy peas

Oil for deep frying

This is a lovely, aromatic way to eat scallops and the good thing is it can be prepared beforehand and refrigerated before cooking for just 8 minutes.

Scallops baked in their shells

Remove the scallops from their shells and clean. You can get the fishmonger to do this but remember to bring home the shells! Scrub the shells then rinse in boiling water and dry.

Put little piles of rock salt or crumpled tin foil into the base of a roasting tin to act as a bed for the shells. Place the deep, rounded shells into the tin and put a spoonful of the sautéed vegetables in the bottom of each. Top with a scallop and then sprinkle over the lardons and mushrooms, which have been sautéed together, and the herbs.

Meanwhile, boil the wine and cream together until reduced by two-thirds and season with lemon juice, salt and pepper. Put a good tablespoon of sauce into each shell, season with rock salt and pop the flat shell back on as a lid. Seal with a strip of pastry, brush with beaten egg and press with a fork to seal and decorate. Bake at 200°C/400°F/Gas Mark 6 for 6 to 8 minutes until the pastry is golden. Serve with a wedge of lemon and use chunks of pastry for dunking.

3 large scallops (dived if possible) per person, in the shell

2 leeks and 2 carrots both cut into thin strips and sautéed in butter for 2 minutes

100g (4oz) smoked bacon lardons

12 shiitake mushrooms, thinly sliced

Fresh chopped chervil and fennel

half a bottle white wine

300ml (10fl oz) whipping cream

Juice of 2 lemons

Salt and pepper

Ready-made puff pastry rolled into thin strips

It doesn't take long to cook a live crab and the difference between freshly cooked crabmeat and any other kind – dressed, frozen or tinned – is like comparing Manchester United with Hambleton Wanderers (2nd XI). Both are football teams but that's where the similarity ends. Freshly cooked crab has the taste of the sea and it is worth the effort. Any good fishmonger should be able to provide live specimens. And always chose a cock crab – the females are often full of roe.

Crab cocktail with avocado, tomato tartare and grapefruit dressing

Bring a large pan of water to a rolling boil, add a cup of salt and drop in the live crab. Bring back to the boil and cook for 14 minutes. Remove and place in a large bowl of iced water to halt the cooking. When cool break off the legs and claws, crack open and carefully pick all the white meat into a bowl. Pull the rounded body of the crab away from the shell, taking care to discard the 'dead men's fingers', which look like grey feathery fronds. Spoon the brown meat from the shell into another bowl and puree. Pick over the meat to check for bits of shell. You should be left with about 300g-450g (12-16oz) of crab.

Mix together the avocado, shredded lettuce, chopped apple, all the white crab meat, 4 tablespoons of brown crabmeat, 4 tablespoons of marie rose sauce, the juice of the lemons and lime and the chives. Chill. In another bowl, combine the tomato dice, basil, shallots, ketchup and vinegar and season to taste.

It is best to assemble this dish on a tray before moving it to a serving plate as it can be a little messy. Place four ring moulds or cutters, 8cm diameter and 4 cm deep (3in x 1.5in) on a tray and fill almost to the top with the crab and avocado mixture. Top with the tomato mixture and smooth the surface. Use a fish slice to move the moulds to the centre of a serving plate and carefully remove the moulds. Dress the salad leaves with the grapefruit dressing and pile a small mound of leaves on top of the cocktail. Decorate the edges of the plate with extra dressing or a drizzle of olive oil.

one large 2 kg (4lb) cock crab

2 avocados, diced

2 heads of little gem lettuce, shredded

3 tablespoons of chopped chives

marie rose sauce – 4 tablespoons each mayonnaise and tomato ketchup mixed together with a dash of Tabasco

2 Granny Smith apples, grated and squeezed of excess liquid

2 lemons

1 lime

8 medium tomatoes, skinned, de-seeded and diced

8 basil leaves, shredded,

2 small shallots, finely chopped

2 tablespoons tomato ketchup

1 tablespoon balsamic vinegar

salad leaves including chicory, radicchio and frisee

grapefruit dressing – 100ml (3fl oz) grapefruit juice, 50ml (1.5fl oz) olive oil and 25ml (1fl oz) water, whisked together

A Dinner Party at
Burghley House

PARTRIDGE TARTLET WITH WILD MUSHROOMS

LOIN OF FALLOW VENISON WITH
ELDERBERRY SAUCE, GALETTE POTATO
AND RED CABBAGE

CAPPUCCINO OF BLACKBERRIES

I've always associated Burghley House in Lincolnshire with the world-famous Horse Trials but it was a trial of a culinary nature that faced me when I stepped into their fantastic Elizabethan kitchen.

It seemed like a good idea at the time.

Burghley is the largest and grandest Elizabethan house in England and remains in the hands of the Cecil family, its latest occupants being Mr Simon and Lady Victoria Leatham. Lady Victoria is also a leading expert on the long-running BBC series, The Antiques Roadshow.

A few hundred years ago the kitchen at Burghley (roughly about the size of a four bedroom house) would have been jam-packed with dozens of staff cooking for the Lord High Treasurer of England, William Cecil.

All I had to help me was my sous-chef and trusty manservant, Julian Carter, Liverpool FC supporter and about as far removed from the trappings of the gentry as you can get. Taking us both into account, a real case of a visit from the hoi polloi.

As I said, it seemed like a good idea. A three-course dinner party for Lady Victoria, her husband Simon and guests, including Hambleton's owner, Tim Hart.

Of course, on television, nothing is as it seems. To start with the producer failed to mention that the kitchens may look great but there's no power in there to cook in the ancient ovens

So it was a case of bringing in my old, battered portable cooker from Hambleton, dressing it up with black drapes so it looked respectable on camera, and hauling in a huge gas container to fire up the rings. I only found out later that Burghley insists on ten million pounds of insurance in case of ... well, it doesn't bear thinking about.

Oven crisis over, I then realised that we couldn't use the kitchen surfaces to prepare food because of their age and value. And all through the cooking sequences various members of household security staff kept an eagle eye on the crew and me as we cooked for the cameras.

The kitchen was unbelievable. There I was, surrounded by massive pots and pans with dozens of gleaming copper moulds, dishes and soup tureens lining the walls. Lady Victoria explained that hundreds of years ago people were very big on soups and squidgy desserts for one simple reason : their teeth were rotten – and in some cases non-existent. They couldn't eat anything that required a bit of chewing. Hence, the tureens and moulds.

Turtle soup was a big favourite at Burghley, and I can tell you it's a bit eerie cooking beneath the turtle skulls that have been embedded in the kitchen wall as a reminder of the dish.

Anyway, back to the present. I'd devised a menu that made the best of the venison on the estate and unusually I put a game starter with a game main course, but the partridge tart was so light that it worked really well. And the dessert – a Cappuccino of Blackberries – is always a conversation piece.

I have to admit that, although on camera, it may look like a civilised, relaxed dinner party with friends, the truth was quite different. We'd consulted Lady Victoria's butler, Jason, about the 'correct' way to proceed but because of the tight filming schedule, Julian and I could only cook two portions of each dish. It looked as though all the guests were tucking into a proper meal but when the cameras stopped rolling, the two portions were passed around the table so everyone could have a taste. At least they seemed to enjoy the day and no-one got indigestion.

For me, it was a real pleasure. The splendour of Burghley is self-evident and if your guide is the delightful and charming Lady Victoria herself what more can you ask?

As we strode through 160 acres of ancient deer park among the oldest Fallow herd in the country, sipped mulberry gin under the very tree the fruit came from and discovered the secrets of the kitchen's old ice house, I began to find myself warming to the aristocratic lifestyle.

I don't know about being 'below stairs', though. I can't imagine how they managed to produce so many elaborate dinners and banquets with such limited facilities.

But I suppose at least the ovens worked.

A DINNER PARTY AT BURGHLEY HOUSE

There are two kinds of partridge – the French, red-legged partridge that is reasonably easy to find and the grey-legged 'English' which is quite scarce. It's hardly surprising that the English rarity is twice the price, but it also has twice the flavour. Distinctive, gamey and intense. Well worth searching out.

Partridge tartlet with wild mushrooms

Gently sweat the shallots, mushrooms and garlic in the butter until the mushroom liquid has evaporated, leaving an intensely flavoured duxelle. Add the Madeira and cream and reduce to a thick, coating consistency. Just before serving add salt, pepper and lemon juice to taste and the chopped tarragon.

Make the salad dressing by whisking all the ingredients together. Dress the leaves and divide between four plates. Add the knob of butter and tablespoon of oil to a hot pan, throw in a sprig of thyme and a crushed clove of garlic and sear the partridge breasts for 2 minutes each side. Rest for 1 minute. Put a pastry case on top of the leaves, fill with the warm mushroom mixture and top with a partridge breast, thinly sliced. Garnish with a sprig of chervil.

Four partridge breasts

Four individual short crust pastry cases

A knob of butter

1 tablespoon vegetable oil

Sprig of thyme

1 garlic clove, crushed

250g (9oz) wild mushrooms

2 shallots, diced

100ml (3fl oz) whipping cream

75g (3oz) butter

100ml (3fl oz) Madeira

lemon juice

fresh tarragon, chopped

salad leaves including frisée, radicchio, rocket and dandelion leaves

4 sprigs of chervil

for the salad dressing:

100ml (3fl oz) fresh squeezed grapefruit juice

50ml (2fl oz) olive oil

25ml (1fl oz water

salt and pepper

4 x 150g (5oz) pieces of loin of venison

3 juniper berries

2 sprigs thyme

1 clove garlic, crushed

1 tablespoon butter

1 tablespoon olive oil

20 baby onions

1 tablespoon butter

1 tablespoon olive oil

150ml (5fl oz) chicken stock

75g (3oz) sugar

3 sprigs thyme

1 garlic clove, crushed

1 tablespoon sherry vinegar

Sprigs of chervil for garnish

1 medium red cabbage

knob of butter

1 tablespoon of olive oil

150g (5oz) blackberries
pureed in a liquidiser and sieved

100ml (3fl oz) balsamic vinegar

100ml (3fl oz) honey

First make a stock by browning the meat trimmings in a large heavy pan. Add the vegetables, alcohol, herbs and spices and reduce the volume by about a third. Pour in enough chicken stock to cover and simmer for 45 minutes, skimming frequently. Strain into a smaller pan and reduce vigorously until you have a thick gravy – about 150ml (5fl oz). You could make the gravy several days before and refrigerate. When ready to serve, reheat and add the berries, seasoning with salt, pepper and lemon juice.

Sweat the shredded cabbage gently in a little oil and butter for one minute. Add the honey, blackberry puree and vinegar and cook until the liquid is slightly reduced and glossy. Season with salt and pepper. This should have a good sweet and sour taste.

For the potatoes, melt the butter and water together and mix in the shredded potato, seasoning well with salt and pepper. Pack the potato into 4 shallow tins, about 10cm x 3cm deep (4in x 1in). Pour over some of the butter and water mixture. Place the tins in a dry, heavy bottomed frying pan or onto a solid hob and cook on a medium heat. As the water evaporates the potato will cook to a buttery, golden brown. Turn when the underside is firm and becoming golden and cook until the galette is soft in the centre and golden on both sides but not too brown or crunchy (that makes it a rosti).

Loin of Fallow Deer with elderberry sauce, galette potato and red cabbage

Prepare the onions by placing them in a heavy pan with a tablespoon each of butter and olive oil and the sugar. Heat until the sugar melts and cook gently until the mixture is caramelised. Add the thyme, garlic, sherry vinegar and chicken stock, stir well and cook on a medium heat until the onions are tender and glazed and the liquid is reduced.

Sear the pieces of venison until golden in the oil and butter. Season with salt and pepper, add the juniper berries, 2 sprigs of thyme and the garlic and cook at 200°C/400°F/Gas Mark 6 for 3 minutes either side. The cooking time depends on the thickness of the loin. Test with a skewer until cooked to your liking.

To assemble the dish, place the potato galette in the centre of a deep dish. Top it with a large tablespoon of red cabbage. Cut the venison loin in half lengthways and place criss-crossed on top of the cabbage. Arrange the onions around the edges of the plate, garnish each onion with a sprig of chervil and spoon the sauce around.

2 large potatoes, coarsely grated

250g (9oz) butter

150ml (5fl oz) water

salt and pepper

For the sauce:

Venison trimmings including bones if possible

2 each – carrots, leeks and celery sticks

Half a head of garlic

4 sprigs of thyme

2 bay leaves

6 juniper berries

1 bottle red wine

half a bottle of port

600ml (20fl oz) strong chicken stock

squeeze lemon juice

salt and pepper

200g (8oz) elderberries (or you could use blackberries or blackcurrants)

This dish always brings a smile to people's faces. Blackberry soup with a spoonful of blackberry sorbet topped by creamy sabayon, all served in a large Cappuccino cup with a couple of chocolates on the side. A very impressive dessert and easy to assemble at the last minute.

A DINNER PARTY AT BURGHLEY HOUSE

Cappuccino of Blackberries

Put the frozen fruit in a pan with all the other soup ingredients. Bring to the boil, turn the heat off and leave to infuse for 6 hours or overnight. Strain through a sieve lined with muslin or through a jelly bag. Sweeten the clear juice with icing sugar to taste and stir in a tablespoon of Crème de Mures. There should be enough to fill each cup three-quarters full. Chill until ice cold

For the sorbet, puree the fresh blackberries in a liquidiser, push through a fine sieve, stir in the juice of a lemon and sweeten to taste with icing sugar. Put into a sorbet maker or pour into a shallow freezer proof dish and freeze for 2-3 hours until slushy. Beat well with a fork to remove the ice crystals and return to the freezer. Repeat at least once more. Both the soup and the sorbet should be prepared beforehand.

Whisk the egg yolks and water in a stainless steel bowl over a pan of simmering water until thick and creamy. Gradually whisk in the sugar and add a dash of Pernod. This should be served warm.

To serve, three-quarters fill each cup with the ice-cold blackberry soup and add a scoop of sorbet. Spoon the sabayon over the top. For an extra fun touch, dry out a handful of halved blackberries in a very low oven until completely hard. Grind to a powder in a coffee grinder and sprinkle over the sabayon. Serve with a teaspoon and 2 chocolates on each saucer.

Blackberry soup:

1 kg (2lbs) frozen blackberries
juice of a lemon
4 star anise
150ml (5fl oz) water
icing sugar to taste
Crème de Mures (blackberry liqueur)

Blackberry sorbet:

450g (1lb) fresh blackberries
icing sugar
juice of a lemon
Sabayon:
3 egg yolks
2 tablespoons sugar
3 tablespoons water
Pernod

32 fresh blackberries to serve
2 chocolates per person

An alternative
Sunday Lunch

MEDITERRANEAN VEGETABLE TERRINE

ROAST SIRLOIN OF BEEF
WITH YORKSHIRE PUDDING, CASSIS ONIONS
AND HORSERADISH HOLLANDAISE

HONEY ROAST SPICED DUCK WITH STIR–FRIED
VEGETABLES AND ORIENTAL POTATOES

I'm in search of Sunday lunch and this certainly proved to be the strangest I've never sat down to. I'm in the heart of Warwickshire watching a long line of Buddhist followers hand over homemade dishes to an abbot and his acolytes. Exotic Thai and Burmese dishes, salads, fruitcake – even egg sandwiches – are all being stacked on top of each other into the monks' huge eating bowls. What a mixture. It's a colourful and bizarre sight and the man who runs this Buddhist hermitage has an equally colourful past – albeit one he's renounced. He's known only as Khemadhammo, but in a past life this quietly-spoken 59-year-old was a National Theatre actor who appeared on stage and in films with greats like Sir Laurence Olivier and Sir Ralph Richardson. Khemadhammo is a Forest Monk, which means he and his followers like to live close to nature. Their beliefs mean they can only eat food that is offered to them and it must be strictly vegetarian – hence this gathering and the filling of the food bowls.

I must confess that I was a bit apprehensive about meeting the monks, probably because I don't really understand their ways. I couldn't give up everything – possessions, family, friends ... and food. In stockinged feet I make my way to their private eating quarters with my personal offering for Sunday lunch. Though I say so myself, it's a stunning

Mediterranean vegetable terrine and it looks a picture on the plate. Khemadhammo graciously accepts it. I can see he appreciates its beauty. Then he upends the plate and the contents plummet into the waiting bowl to join the sweet and sour sauces, the fruitcake, and the egg sandwiches. Who am I – a simple cook – to argue with thousands of years of tradition? Try my vegetable terrine, but I suggest you leave out the egg sandwiches.

On leaving Warwickshire it was on to the West Midlands to find out what Birmingham's Chinatown had to offer. Chinese restaurants always seems to be packed on Sundays – usually with the Chinese themselves. Traditionally it's a constant stream of tasty little morsels called dim sum. I spent a great day in Birmingham finding out how the Chinese like to eat on a Sunday and getting some inspiration for a Chinese-style lunch to cook back at Hambleton.

First I paid a visit to Mr Wing Yip's Chinese superstore in Birmingham. Inspiration hit me from all sides. The place covers seven acres and you won't be surprised to hear that it is the biggest and best in Britain. Mr Yip is one of Europe's top specialist food importers and at the last count more than 20 countries were supplying his superstore. It was a fantastic place with literally thousands upon thousands of different product lines. Take prawns. (I did).

Mr Yip proudly pointed out the 45 different varieties in stock.

I did get a bit carried away. Alongside the prawns, Chinese spices, vegetables, exotic sauces, fresh fish all found their way into my trolley. I have to stop after buying a crispy, brown whole Peking duck, complete with head and beak. I pass on the salmon heads, though. Even though Mr Yip assures me these are a delicacy and reserved for the honoured head of the household.

But back to Sunday lunch and on to the vast China Court Restaurant where I discover that 'dim' means small and 'sum' means 'lovingly made' – a very apt description. The dim sum chef patiently teaches me how to make these mouth-watering delicacies but I can't take my eyes off what's happening elsewhere in the kitchen. They're in the middle of preparing a wedding feast for a bride who is expected at any minute. It's controlled chaos. Too many lobsters to count are being split in half (live) and deep fried and a dozen suckling pigs are roasting away in one corner – it's just how you'd imagine a busy Chinese restaurant to be. Then the bride sweeps into the restaurant and they move up a gear. She looks beautiful but I was surprised to see she was wearing a traditional white wedding dress. Apparently Chinese brides wear red but, just as their food has become westernised, so have many other traditions.

It was a complete contrast to that frantic kitchen when I visited farmer Richard Vaughan at his 500-year-old farmhouse in Herefordshire's Wye Valley to remind myself of a traditional British Sunday lunch. There's a warm, homely atmosphere in the farmhouse kitchen and a gargantuan sirloin of Longhorn beef roasting in the oven. For a change, Sunday lunch is being cooked for me and it doesn't get more traditional than this. A roaring log fire, a bottle of fine Claret and someone else doing the cooking. Heaven. This 'someone else' knows about beef too. Richard can talk for hours about his beloved Longhorn cattle and the marvellous beef they produce. And he does. He used to farm mass-produced beef but all that changed when he rang the slaughterhouse to get them to put a piece of his own beef to one side for him and was told: 'You don't want to eat that rubbish..!' So he changed his farming methods, concentrated on rare breeds, quality and flavour. And now his beef is some of the most sought-after in Britain.

I love a traditional roast dinner, but I have my own particular way of doing it. Little individual roasts, perfect Yorkshire Puddings that don't need smoking fat so hot that you have to call the fire brigade, a great gravy and a little surprise tucked away in the puddings.

All I need now is an afternoon nap.

This makes approximately 15 slices.

1.75 litre (3pt) terrine mould

4 large aubergines to line the mould

600ml (1pt) water

100ml (3fl oz)honey

150ml (5fl oz)) white wine vinegar

2 star anise

salt and pepper

For the coulis:

**20 large juicy plum tomatoes,
halved and de-seeded**

150ml (5fl oz) olive oil

14 leaves of gelatine

3 tablespoons balsamic vinegar

For the filling:

**5 large red peppers, cut in quarters
lengthways, peeled and de-seeded**

**5 large yellow peppers,
prepared the same way**

**4 medium aubergines
cut into 2.5 cm (1in) discs**

**8 tinned artichoke hearts,
well drained and wiped dry**

small jar of tapenade

20 basil leaves

4 cloves of garlic

6 sprigs of thyme

300ml (10fl oz)) vegetable oil

300ml (10fl oz)) of olive oil

3 tablespoons balsamic vinegar

150ml (5fl oz) of water

300ml (5fl oz) white wine vinegar

I make this every week at Hambleton and it's really popular. The colours and tastes are so bright and vibrant that it really gets the taste buds going. It's one of those versatile dishes that can be served on its own as a starter or with goat's cheese, red mullet, prawns or scallops as a more substantial course. It looks complicated but it's not. Basically, you start out with a big tray of raw ingredients and end up with a big tray of cooked ingredients, and then you just need to layer it correctly. The terrine is lined with aubergine skins and they must be blanched in fast-boiling liquid in order to turn them bright purple – otherwise they go brown. Of course, if you're going to throw it all into a monk's bowl I don't suppose it really matters...

Mediterranean vegetable terrine

Start with the coulis. This will set the terrine. Cook the tomatoes over a high heat with 150ml (5fl oz) of olive oil until reduced to a pulp. Season with salt and pepper. Add 150ml (5fl oz) of balsamic vinegar and press through a coarse sieve. You will need a litre (34 fl oz) of juice and this will depend on the size and juiciness of the tomatoes. Soak the gelatine leaves in a little cold water until soft and jelly-like. Warm a small amount of tomato liquid in a saucepan and add the squeezed-out gelatine leaves and dissolve, then whisk into the rest of the tomato coulis. Season.

Cut the 4 large aubergines into half and then quarters, lengthways. Remove as much flesh as possible leaving just the skins. Boil together the water, honey, white wine vinegar and star anise and when it is boiling vigorously, throw in the skins and keep the liquid fast-boiling for 4 minutes. The skins will turn bright purple and have a sweet and sour flavour. Remove and lay on kitchen paper.

Put the red peppers and yellow peppers into two separate pans and just cover with vegetable oil. Add 150ml (5fl oz) of white wine vinegar to each pan, a whole garlic clove and 3 sprigs of thyme. Cook gently until the peppers are tender but still retain their shape – the yellow peppers for about 15 minutes and the red peppers for five minutes longer. Remove the peppers from the pan and place on kitchen paper.

Heat 300ml (10fl oz) of olive oil in a frying pan that can go into the oven and fry the aubergine discs until golden brown on each side. Sprinkle with 4 sprigs of rosemary, 2 garlic cloves, 3 tablespoons of balsamic vinegar and 150ml (5fl oz) of water then cover and cook at 200°C/400°F/Gas Mark 6 for about 6 minutes. Remove and put alongside the peppers.

Fill the hollows of each artichoke heart with a teaspoon of tapenade.

Now comes the easy bit! Oil the terrine and triple-line with cling film leaving plenty hanging over the edge. Line the sides and the base of the terrine with the aubergine skins, shiny side down, again leaving some hanging over the edge.

Spoon a thin layer of coulis (about a ladleful) into the base followed by a layer of aubergine discs. Layer the red and yellow peppers, with coulis between each layer, and finish with a layer of coulis. Now add a layer of artichokes, tapenade-side down, followed by another layer of coulis and the basil leaves.

Finish with more coulis, the remaining aubergine discs and a final layer of coulis. This should be level with the top of the terrine. Turn the aubergine skins over the top of the terrine, cover with cling film and refrigerate for 24 hours.

Roast sirloin of beef with Yorkshire Pudding, Cassis onions and horseradish Hollandaise

If you don't want to cook a big joint, or there are just two of you, these individual roasts are perfect. The pieces of sirloin must be cut like a thick fillet steak. Ask your butcher to cut a double-thick sirloin steak, at least 7cm (2.5in) thick. Trim off any fat and gristle and then cut the steak into two chunky pieces. I serve the roasts inside a Yorkshire Pudding and I'm afraid I disagree with many cooks who insist the only way to make puddings rise properly is to pour the batter into red hot tins full of spitting fat. I think that method spoils the pudding, making it blister and rise unevenly. Horseradish is the traditional accompaniment to roast beef

but I often find it is too hot and makes me sneeze. This combination of fiery horseradish and creamy Hollandaise still retains a bit of 'bite' but is much nicer. The roasts cook on top of thick slices of onion, which then flavour a creamy gravy. I'd serve baby carrots, glazed shallots and cooked baby beets on the side.

44

First make the batter. Break the eggs into the flour and salt. Beat to a paste and gradually whisk in the milk. Warm 4 individual non-stick Yorkshire pudding tins, 10cm x 2.5cm deep (4in x 1in), in the oven but do not overheat. Put a tablespoon of oil into each tin and a ladle of batter and cook for 15-20 minutes at 200°C/400°F/Gas Mark 6. This method will give you puddings that are well-risen and even, with a nice hollow for the meat.

Puree the blackcurrants in a liquidiser and sieve. Sweat the finely sliced onions in the butter and oil until soft and translucent but not coloured. This could take half an hour, over a very gentle heat. Remove from the heat and stir in 4 tablespoons of the blackcurrant puree.

Make the Hollandaise by beating the eggs with the water in a stainless steel bowl over simmering water until doubled in volume. Gradually add the melted butter in a thin stream, whisking all the time until thick and creamy. Remove from the heat, stir in the horseradish and season.

Put 2 tablespoons each of oil and butter into a hot pan and sear the sirloins for a minute or two on each side until golden brown. Season and slip a thick slice of onion under each piece of meat. This protects the meat from drying out and helps flavour the gravy. Cook in the oven at 200°C/400°F/Gas Mark 6 for 3-4 minutes each side, depending on the thickness of the meat. Remove the meat to a warm plate, cover and leave to rest for at least 2 minutes while you finish the gravy.

De-glaze the pan with a tablespoon of sherry vinegar, breaking up the onions and scraping up the meat residue. Add the mustard, wine, stock and cream and bring to the boil, reducing the gravy by half, then season with salt, pepper and lemon juice and stir in the tarragon.

To serve, put a large tablespoon of onions into each pudding and top with a tablespoon of horseradish hollandaise. Slice the meat through the middle and arrange the two slices at an angle on top of the Hollandaise. Pour the sauce into the centre of a deep plate, arrange the vegetables around the plate and put the filled Yorkshire pudding on top.

4 x 175g (6oz) chunky medallions of sirloin

1 large Spanish onion cut into 4 thick slices

2 tablespoons butter

2 tablespoons olive oil

1 tablespoon sherry vinegar

1 tablespoon grain mustard

half a bottle of red wine

200ml (7fl oz) chicken stock

125ml (4fl oz) whipping cream

lemon juice

chopped fresh tarragon

5 eggs

250g (9 oz) flour

450ml (15fl oz) milk

teaspoon of salt

2 large Spanish onions, finely sliced

75g (3oz) butter

l tablespoon olive oil

250g (9 oz) fresh or frozen blackcurrants

3 egg yolks

200ml (7fl oz) water

250g (9oz) butter, melted

125g (4oz) of hot creamed horseradish

salt and pepper

The sweet and sour ingredients in this recipe – ginger, star anise, citrus juice, honey and balsamic vinegar – cut through the fattiness of the duck and leave it tender, golden and beautifully glazed. It looks impressive served on a big oval platter of stir-fried vegetables with the oriental potatoes on the side in a Chinese wooden steamer – the kind that is used for dim sum in Chinese restaurants.

2.5 kg (5lb) duck

3 sticks of lemon grass

the juices of a lemon, lime and orange (save the zest for the glaze)

3cm (1in) cube fresh ginger, sliced

3 star anise

3 sprigs of thyme

4 tablespoons vegetable oil

salt and pepper

20 new potatoes, Jersey Royals if possible

1 stick lemon grass

3cm (1in) cube fresh ginger, sliced

Honey roast spiced duck with stir-fried vegetables and oriental potatoes

Score the duck skin in a criss-cross pattern with a sharp knife to release the fat. Seal slowly on top of the oven in a hot, dry pan until golden brown. Remove the duck to a roasting tin and tuck the lemon grass, ginger, star anise and thyme around the bird. Pour in the citrus juices and brush the vegetable oil over the top of the duck. Season and roast at 200°C/400°F/Gas Mark 6, basting frequently, for 45 minutes. Remove and rest for at least 10 minutes.

Turn the potatoes into the pan in which the duck was browned, add the lemon grass and ginger and roast with the duck for 20 minutes. Boil all the glaze ingredients together for a few minutes until syrupy. Stir fry the vegetables in a little vegetable oil and soy sauce and pile onto a large platter. Put the duck in the centre, pour over the glossy glaze and carve at the table. Serve the potatoes in the wooden steamer, sprinkled with rock salt.

The glaze:

4 tablespoons soy sauce

4 tablespoons balsamic vinegar

150g (6oz) honey

2 star anise

2 tablespoons liquorice powder
(optional – try a Chinese supermarket)

2 tablespoons Chinese 5-spice powder

zest of an orange and a lime

2 sticks of lemon grass

3cm (1in) cube fresh ginger, sliced

a selection of vegetables which could include pak choi, bean sprouts, shredded carrots, broccoli, mange tout, sliced chillies and cashew nuts

NORTHFIELD FARM

BRITISH MIDDLEWHITE PORK
HIGHLAND SHORTHORN & BELTED GALLOWAY BEEF
GALWAY LAMB
TESSA'S COOKED MEALS
DRY-CURED OAK SMOKED BACON

WE HOPE TO BE HERE
NEXT WEEK.
PLEASE SUPPORT
BRITISH FARMERS
+ PRODUCE IN ANY
WAY YOU CAN!

The French Connection

ASSIETTE OF MARKET FISH

CHICKEN IN A SALT PASTRY CRUST
WITH WILD RICE AND BABY LEEKS

PEAR PAIN PERDU WITH CRÈME ANGLAISE
AND CARAMEL SAUCE

Most people look forward to a holiday for the sun or the beach. Maybe a chance to see the sights or visit a museum. I love all of that, but the chances are that my first port of call, wherever I am, is to see what the local market has to offer.

Fish markets in Spain; tiny piazzas in Italy bursting at the seams with fresh fruit and vegetables and, of course, France, where any little town or village worth its salt still regards market day in the local square as the focal point of the week for fresh food and new gossip.

The French have clung to their love affair with local produce. Food, of course, has been elevated to a religion and there's no denying that the number of markets and the choice and quality of produce on those market is outstanding. But I must say, in recent years, we British have been showing signs of 'life after supermarkets', with the growth of farmers' markets and the like. They've been springing up all over the place, and not too many miles away from my kitchen at Hambleton, I've now got the choice of quite a few on a weekly basis.

The original idea of a farmers' market came from the United States to enable local producers to sell direct to the public. Now places like Melton Mowbray – the home of the world famous pork pies – have fallen in love with the idea. Local farmers like Jan McCourt, who supplies me with Dexter beef, can be found there, selling and preaching about the need to know where our food comes from. Jan started his rare breed business when his career as a bond dealer in London came to an unexpected full stop. Now he farms 250 acres in Rutland and ironically finds himself back in London every weekend at yet another local market – Borough Market – selling his beef and pork.

Borough's a truly amazing place and on a Sunday morning has become a magnet for food lovers. It's real slice of old London: the rumble of trains overhead; ancient wrought ironwork in every nook and cranny and, in the middle of it all, truly passionate producers of top-class meat, fish, cheese, bread, fruit and vegetables.

We've got a way to go in our approach to fresh food but, to my mind, Borough Market and places like it show we're on the right road. Everyone I spoke to there seemed to have an almost religious fervour about their own particular speciality. And what a pleasure to be allowed to touch and feel some of the goods on offer. For me, a million miles away from some unpleasant memories of dealers at Covent Garden who considered their wares far too precious to be prodded by a mere chef.

Of course, I can't talk about markets without mentioning my local one at Uppingham, which is twinned with Caudebec in Normandy. Caudebec also has a market and I visited both.

The choice in Caudebec was stunning – the variety of fish and shellfish on the market was particularly outstanding. Of course, the town

isn't far from the big Channel fishing ports, hence the selection – though I suspect a lot of the fish had come from the other side of the Channel (but that's another issue).

Fresh local fruit, vegetables, poultry and regional cheeses – they were all on offer. And all in that inimitable French style: rickety kitchen tables had been set up by little old women selling a few free range chickens and ducks; creamy ladles of fromage frais and fromage blanc from a local farm were being dispensed from huge Tupperware containers and a knarled old farmer was offering a few kilos of knobbly potatoes and bunches of garlic.

As good as Uppingham's market is – and there's also a great fish stall there every Friday – it's those little producers that we don't seem to get on England's market squares any more. I'm told by locals who supply me at Hambleton that health and environmental regulations would prevent them selling chickens and cheese the way they do on Caudebec market. But one of those little old French ladies told me they have exactly the same regulations in France but choose to interpret them ... how can I put this? Loosely.

In Caudebec I lost count of the number of boulangeries where the choice was vast – from the basic baguette to the most elaborate fruit tartlet. The French are renowned for their love of bread, and households often shop twice a day

for fresh bread, but then the English have always liked a good, tasty loaf. So why is it so difficult to buy one?

Some supermarkets are improving, with a bigger selection of better bread, but whatever happened to the independent baker? At least Uppingham can hold its head up with the French on that score. The local baker is Richard Baines and his family has been baking bread in the town for more than 130 years, in the same old stone ovens. The day I visited it was just like the Hovis television commercial as I followed that fantastic smell of baking bread around Uppingham and ended up in the 17th century townhouse in which Richard lives and works. Quite frankly, Richard's bread really is a taste of an England we once knew ... but have sadly forgotten. I felt like a kid let loose in a sweet shop.

Just down the road from the bakers, I met Dave and Kath Corbett who have done their own bit for the local food scene by bringing back a lost Rutland cheese. They've called it the Lydington Slipcote after their home village (though the original was the Whissendine Slipcote). The French are quite rightly proud of their Livarots and their Camemberts, but it's thanks to enthusiasts like Dave and Kath that we can be equally proud of own own cheese heritage.

So, Uppingham stands up pretty well to its French counterpart. We're getting there.

As far as I'm concerned this way of cooking fish is simply the best. As long as the fish is absolutely spanking fresh. It hardly takes any cooking time and the light sauce tastes of the sea. Just serve it with good, crusty bread to mop up the juices and maybe a dish of garlic mayonnaise. It's hard to be specific over which fish to use. It has to be what is fresh on the day. In an ideal world...

Assiette of market fish

Scale and fillet the fish. Leave the skin on the red mullet. Cut the fillets into pieces of about 10cm x 5cm (4in x 2in) to give each person an equal portion.

Heat a tablespoon of oil in a non-stick pan and lay the fillets in the one layer. Sear for 30 seconds on each side. Remove from the heat. Heat a tablespoon of oil in another pan and stir in the garlic and thyme. Throw the shellfish into the pan and pour over the white wine. Cover and steam for about a minute until the shells open, discarding any that don't. Then pour the shellfish and all the strained juices into the other pan containing the fish. Add the butter, 150ml (4fl oz) of water, the chives and the tomatoes and mix together over a moderate heat for 1 minute. Divide the fish between four deep soup plates, pour over the sauce and dive in with the bread.

675g (1.5lb) Red Mullet, on the bone

450g (1lb) Dover Sole, on the bone

20 clams, scrubbed
(I like Palourdes, Venus or Almonds)

12 mussels, scrubbed

4 scallops, cleaned

4 large raw prawns, shell on

2 glasses of white wine

1 clove garlic, crushed

2 sprigs thyme

4 tomatoes, skinned, de–seeded and diced

juice of half a lemon

2 tablespoons olive oil

50g (2oz) butter

1 tablespoon chives, chopped

salt and pepper

This is a really fun dish to serve. The salt crust (which isn't eaten) can be cracked open at the table to reveal moist, juicy, aromatic chicken. I cook this at Hambleton and we go to a lot of trouble to form the crust into a chicken shape with wings and a little pastry head. It makes for an impressive presentation so have a go, but don't worry if you're not very artistic, it'll taste just as good. We use the 'front' or 'crown' of the bird, basically the two breasts on the bone with the legs, wings and backbone removed. You can then use these to make the sauce. A more convenient choice at home could be a whole poussin for each person or a pigeon or partridge. That way you can leave everyone to crack open their own portion at the table and lift their bird out onto a bed of wild rice and leeks. And if you think this sounds difficult, spare a thought for me last Christmas. At Hambleton we cooked all our turkeys this way. What we hadn't thought about was how to get the beasts into the oven. They only just fitted. But everyone was impressed and it certainly kept the meat juicy.

Chicken in a salt pastry crust with wild rice and baby leeks

First make the pastry crust. Mix the egg whites into the flour and salt and add enough cold water to make a stiff, dry dough. This must not be at all wet. Set aside to rest.

For the sauce, remove the wings and backbone from the chickens and chop. Remove the legs and leave them whole. Put them all into a large saucepan with 2 chopped onions, the bay leaf and rosemary and barely cover with water. Bring to the boil and simmer gently for 40 minutes, skimming constantly to remove impurities and fat. Strain and reduce the liquid by two-thirds to leave about half a pint of strong chicken stock. Remove from the heat and add the dried mushrooms, leaving them to reconstitute for about 30 minutes. In another pan bring the Madeira and white wine to the boil, reduce by a third, then add the stock, mushrooms and the whipping cream and simmer until the sauce has a velvety consistency. Strain into another pan, wash the mushrooms well, chop finely and put back into the sauce.

Prepare the chicken crowns – or whole individual birds – by stuffing the rosemary, garlic and bay between the flesh and the skin on the breast. Roll the pastry into a circle, roughly twice the size of the chicken and fold it up and around the bird into a neat, chicken-shaped parcel. Seal the pastry edges with water.

Now's the time to do any creative bits with the pastry trimmings before brushing the parcels with beaten egg and sprinkling rock salt all over. Place on a baking sheet and cook at 200°C/400°F/Gas Mark 6 until golden brown. Test after 45 minutes by pushing a metal skewer through the pastry and right into the chicken flesh. If it comes out hot the chicken is cooked, if not, leave for a further 10 minutes.

Crack open the chicken at the table and serve with wild rice, baby leeks and the mushroom and Madeira sauce.

2 x 1.6kg chickens – corn-fed, free-range and organic if possible

a handful of fresh rosemary, a few garlic cloves and 4 bay leaves

2 medium onions, chopped

1 bay leaf

2 sprigs rosemary

100g (4oz) dried wild mushrooms

200ml (7fl oz) Madeira

200ml (7fl oz) white wine

150ml (5fl oz) whipping cream

450g (1lb) flour

225g (8oz) kitchen salt

3 egg whites

cold water

2 eggs, beaten

rock salt

Wild rice, 75-100g (3-4ozs) per person

20 baby leeks

Really just a posh version of eggy bread. A very posh version. A crispy, golden brioche base is topped with a perfectly poached whole pear and served with two sauces – Crème Anglaise and caramel sauce. The pear can be warm but try it chilled – fantastic with the warm sauces. We use wax tip pears, which aren't a variety but a way of conserving the pear at its best. Pears rot from the stalk down into the centre, so when the pears are perfectly ripe the suppliers seal the end of the stalks with a blob of hot, red wax. This helps keeps them from becoming overripe. You can use any good, ripe, tasty pear. Why perdu? It means 'lost' in French and refers to using up stale bread.

Pear Pain Perdu with Crème Anglaise and caramel sauce

Put all the ingredients for the poaching liquor into a pan large enough to take all the pears in a single layer. Dissolve the sugar gently, then boil for 5 minutes to make a light poaching syrup. Add the pears when the liquid is boiling rapidly and simmer for 20-30 minutes depending on the ripeness of the fruit. Test with a skewer. The pears must be very tender but still retain their shape. Cool in the syrup.

Make the Crème Anglaise by whisking together the eggs and sugar until pale and fluffy. Bring the milk, cream, vanilla pods and seeds to the boil then add the eggs and sugar, mixing well. Remove from the heat and continue stirring until the mixture thickens to a light, custardy consistency.

Start the caramel sauce by melting the sugar in a pan with just a tablespoon of water over a high heat to achieve burnt sugar. This gives the sauce a good caramel flavour. Ideally use a sugar thermometer – it's ready at 180°C/350°F. If you don't have a thermometer, you must be very careful. Burn the sugar too much and it will be bitter, too little and it will just taste of sugar. When the sugar is perfectly burnt, remove from the heat and add the Calvados. Take care, as the mixture should bubble fiercely. Then whisk in the cream and the caramel sauce is finished.

To serve, soak the slices of brioche in a little crème Anglaise for a couple of minutes and fry in butter until golden brown on both sides. Drain on kitchen paper and place in the centre of a plate. Top with a poached pear, either chilled or re-heated in the poaching liquid and serve with the two sauces poured around.

4 large wax tip pears, peeled

For the poaching liquor:

1.2 litres (2pts) water

900g (2lbs) granulated sugar

2 vanilla pods, split

2 sticks cinnamon

3 star anise

zest and juice of 2 lemons, 2 limes and 2 oranges

For the Crème Anglaise:

500ml (17fl oz) milk, full cream or semi-skimmed

250ml (8fl oz) double cream

1 vanilla pod, split

6 egg yolks

125g (5oz) caster sugar

For the caramel sauce:

450g (1lb) granulated sugar

100ml (3fl oz) Calvados

300ml (10fl oz) whipping cream

Four square-cut, thick slices of crustless brioche

Large knob of butter

Six Dinner Party Menus

Menu One

Ragout of Wild Mushrooms

Rabbit Pot au Feu

Pear Tarte Tatin

Try to use as many varieties of wild mushrooms as possible – we use Jews Ears, wood blewitts and oysters, all picked by Barry from the woods around Hambleton. Barry also provides us with rabbits for the pot, which reminds me of an hilarious day's filming. Barry prefers to ferret for rabbits rather than shoot them because there's no lead shot to damage the meat. So off we go one freezing February morning with Barry, a former mining mate from Nuneaton in tow, and Barry's elderly brother whom, he claims, used to be a useful winger with West Bromwich Albion in the Forties. A likely story. It was like a scene from The Good, The Bad and The Ugly as the three amigos covered the rabbit holes with nets after sending the ferrets underground. But it worked. As the rabbits bolted up the hole away from the ferrets they're despatched with a swift blow from Barry's brother and we're off back to the kitchen.

Ragout of wild mushrooms

Boil or steam the asparagus spears until tender. Refresh in iced water. Heat the oil and butter in a pan and cook the shallots and garlic until translucent, but not coloured.
Cut the mushrooms into large pieces and add to the pan. Stir for 30 seconds then add the Madeira and reduce for 2 minutes. Add the chicken stock and reduce by half.
Stir in the cream, butter, asparagus, tomatoes and tarragon and warm through. Taste and season with salt and pepper. Serve the ragout over pasta cooked al dente.

1 garlic clove, crushed
1 shallot, finely chopped
450g (1lb) mixed mushrooms, wild if possible
12 asparagus spears
4 tomatoes, skinned and diced
50g (2oz) unsalted butter
1 tablespoon olive oil
Fresh tagliatelle (according to your appetite)
300ml (9fl oz) chicken stock
50g (2oz) unsalted butter
100ml (3fl oz) whipping cream
100ml (3fl oz) white wine
100ml (3fl oz) Madeira
2 tablespoons tarragon, chopped

Rabbits reared for the table have a very mild flavour, one-step above chicken, whereas wild rabbits are completely different – very gamey and with a good texture. Try to find a wild rabbit for this robust casserole.

Rabbit Pot au Feu

Cut the carrots, swede and leeks into rough chunks. Leave the shallots whole and tear off the cabbage leaves. Sear the rabbit portions in the olive oil in a large casserole, adding the garlic, bay leaf and thyme. Tuck the sausage and bacon, both whole, around the rabbit, followed by the vegetables. Fry for a few minutes until lightly caramelised then add the vinegar and reduce for 2 minutes. Add the white wine and reduce for a further 2 minutes. Now add the stock, mustard and pearl barley and season with salt and pepper. Transfer the dish to the oven at 180°C/350°F/Gas Mark 4 for approximately 1-1.5 hours until the meat is tender.

To serve, slice the bacon and sausage into hearty chunks and divide all the meat and vegetables between four large bowls and spoon over the juices.

legs and saddles of two rabbits

1 smoked sausage, preferably morteaux

450g (1lb) streaky smoked belly bacon in one piece

2 tablespoons olive oil

2 carrots

1 swede

4 potatoes

2 leeks

8 shallots

1 bulb fennel cut into quarters

half a cabbage

half a bulb of garlic

100g (4oz) pearl barley

1.2 litres (2pts) chicken stock

4 tablespoons grain mustard

1 bay leaf

4 sprigs thyme

Bottle dry white wine

100ml (3fl oz) white wine vinegar

Pear Tarte Tatin

Peel the pears, cut in half lengthways and core. Place in water acidulated with a little lemon juice to prevent discolouration, until ready to use. Put the sugar and water in a pan and heat gently until the sugar dissolves and then caramelises. Carefully whisk in the butter and pour into a shallow ovenproof, non-stick pan approximately 15cm (6 in) in diameter. Add the cinnamon, star anise and vanilla pod and arrange the pears, flat side uppermost, on top. Allow to cool. Roll the pastry out to 3mm thickness and cut a circle slightly larger than the pan. Place it over the pears, tucking in the edges. Pierce several holes in the pastry to allow steam to escape. Cook the tatin at 190°/375°/Gas Mark 5 for approximately 25-30 minutes until golden brown. To serve, carefully turn out on to a plate and serve with ice cream.

(Serves One)

2 ripe pears

100g (4oz) puff pastry

100g (4oz) sugar

50g (2oz) unsalted butter

300ml (10fl oz) water

1 cinnamon stick

1 star anise

1 vanilla pod

Ice cream of your choice – caramel or vanilla work particularly well

Menu Two

Hambleton Salad with Truffle Oil Dressing

Dexter Beef with a Horseradish Crust & Rosti Potatoes

Passion Fruit Souffle

A few years ago I was up to my neck in the kitchen with 50 covers for lunch when a chap turned up at the kitchen door with a sirloin of beef under his arm. For me it was a bit like love at first sight. Not for the man. For the sirloin. I discovered it was Dexter beef. And when I tasted a sliver, there and then, I was completely won over. It's just how beef should taste, with a beautiful intensity of flavour. The man who introduced me to the Dexter was Jan McCourt, an investment banker turned farmer, who farms 250 acres of prime Rutland and owns the largest herd of miniature Dexter cattle in the country.

Hambleton Salad
with Truffle Oil Dressing

Place the egg yolk in a bowl and gradually whisk in the vegetable oil. Whisk in the vinegar and water, followed by the truffle oil, grain mustard and seasoning. Set aside.

Cook all the vegetables in boiling water until tender then refresh in iced water and dry. Place them in a bowl and season with a dash of white wine vinegar, a squeeze of lemon juice, salt and pepper and a drizzle of olive oil.

Place the salad leaves in a bowl with half the herbs and dress lightly with a few spoonfuls of vinaigrette. To serve, assemble the salad leaves on a plate and arrange the vegetables, halved eggs, croutons and herbs around them. Drizzle over the dressing and finish with a few shavings of Parmesan.

8 each – baby carrots, leeks, asparagus

cherry tomatoes and turnips

4 baby artichokes

4 quails eggs, boiled for 3.5 minutes, cooled and shelled

a handful of fresh herbs –
parsley, chervil and snipped chives

salad leaves including rocket
and textured leaves

Parmesan

croutons

squeeze lemon juice

dash white wine vinegar

Vinaigrette:

1 egg yolk

150ml (5fl oz) vegetable oil

1 tablespoon grain mustard

1 tablespoon white wine vinegar

1 tablespoon water

2 tablespoons truffle oil or walnut oil

salt and pepper

Dexter beef with a horseradish crust and rosti potato

Finely grate the potatoes and mix with the butter and water. Pack into 4 shallow tins, 10cm x 3cm deep (4in x 1in). Pour over some of the butter and water mixture. Place the tins into a dry, heavy bottomed pan or directly on a solid hob and cook on a medium heat. As the water evaporates the potato will cook to a buttery, crisp, golden brown. Take care not to over-brown. Turn the rostis to cook the undersides.

To make the crust, put the baked bread slices into a bowl and add the horseradish, mustard, peppercorns, cream and fresh tarragon and crunch up with your hands until it is roughly mixed.

Now seal the steaks in a hot pan with a dash of virgin olive oil, a knob of butter and season with salt and pepper. When the surface of the beef has caramelised, smear the top with a little grain mustard and mould the crust mix on top. Slip a thick slice of raw potato under the steak (this protects the meat from overcooking). Cook for 6-7 minutes at 200°C/400°F/Gas Mark 6. Discard the potatoes and deglaze the pan with a glass of red wine and a dash of water and whisk in a good knob of butter to make a simple gravy.

This is good served on a bed of cooked, shredded cabbage placed in the centre of a deep plate. Put the rosti on top of the cabbage, then the steak on top. Chunks of carrots and caramelised shallots go well. Drizzle with the pan juices.

4 x 175g (6oz) steaks of Dexter beef fillet

4 thick slices of raw potato

100g (4oz) butter

1 tablespoon grain mustard

dash balsamic vinegar

2 large potatoes, coarsely grated

250g (9oz) melted butter, mixed with an equal volume of water and seasoned with salt and pepper

8 slices of crustless bread, baked in a very low oven until crisp and golden.

4 tablespoons each horseradish sauce, grain mustard and green peppercorns

8 tablespoons single cream

teaspoon of tarragon

Passion Fruit Soufflé

Remove the pulp from the passion fruits and liquidise for 30 seconds. Mix with a dash of orange juice and sugar to taste. Sieve to remove the seeds. Smear the insides of the ramekins with butter and coat lightly with sugar. Place the passion fruit juice in a pan and warm. Dissolve the cornflour in a little water and slowly add to the passion fruit juice, mixing over a low heat with a wooden spoon until it thickens. Take off the heat. Put the egg whites into a perfectly clean bowl and whisk to the soft peak stage. Start adding the sugar gradually as you continue to whisk, until the mixture has doubled in volume. Fold the egg whites through the passion fruit juice mixture until they are incorporated evenly. Fill each ramekin dish, smooth the tops and cook in a hot oven, 200°C/400°F/Gas Mark 6 for 8 minutes. Serve immediately.

4 ramekin dishes

200ml (7fl oz) passion fruit juice (approx. 12–15 fruits)

the juice of an orange

15g (0.5oz) cornflour

8 egg whites

75g (3oz) sugar

Extra sugar for dusting

Menu Three

Trout Niçoise

Loin of Lamb with a Spring Salad & Balsamic Dressing

Chocolate Tart with Bananas, Raspberries & Vanilla Ice Cream

Until I started filming Wild About Food my two main pastimes, outside of cooking, were golf and supporting Leicester City Football Club – neither guaranteed to calm the nerves. But then I discovered trout fishing when Barry and my brother, Andrew, and I went out onto Rutland Water to catch the fish for this menu. Since then fishing has become a bit of a passion and with the lake literally on Hambleton's doorstep, it's great to be able to get away from it all just beyond my kitchen door. This menu would be perfect for a summer dinner party – a light and flavoursome starter, perfectly cooked lamb with a real surprise ingredient, deep-fried leeks, and everyone's favourite dessert – chocolate.

Trout Niçoise

Cook the green beans and refresh in iced water. Boil the potatoes until tender. Sieve the tomato seeds to extract as much juice as possible. Heat the olive oil, add the tomatoes and cook for 2-3 minutes. Add the tomato juices to the pan and stew for a few minutes until soft but not mushy. Then stir in the shredded basil leaves and season with salt, pepper, balsamic vinegar and tomato ketchup to taste. Heat two tablespoons of olive oil in a non-stick frying pan and fry the trout fillets for 2 minutes each side, seasoning with salt and pepper and a squeeze of lemon juice. Warm the olives, green beans and potatoes in a pan with enough virgin olive oil to add a glossy sheen. You may need to add a few dashes of water.

Divide the warm tomatoes between four plates and place a trout fillet on top of each. Arrange the beans, olives and potatoes around the trout and sprinkle with fennel.

4 medium trout fillets, boned and skinned

2 tablespoons olive oil

8 plum tomatoes, skinned, de-seeded and halved

200ml (7fl oz) virgin olive oil

squeeze of lemon juice

40 green beans

16 baby new potatoes

24 black olives, halved and stoned

a sprinkling of chopped fennel leaves

a handful of basil leaves, shredded

1 teaspoon balsamic vinegar

1 teaspoon tomato ketchup

Loin of lamb with Spring salad and balsamic dressing

Place all the vinaigrette ingredients in a bowl and whisk together.

Deep-fry the leeks, preferably in olive oil, until golden brown and crispy. Drain on kitchen paper and season with salt. Boil or steam the potatoes and asparagus until tender and keep warm. Sear the lamb pieces on all sides in olive oil then add the garlic cloves, whole tomatoes and rosemary and season with salt and pepper. Once this starts to caramelise, place in the oven at 200°/400°/Gas Mark 6 for 8-10 minutes for medium. Remove from the oven and rest for 2 minutes in a warm place.

Toss the salad leaves and herbs in the vinaigrette. Place in the centre of large, deep plates and arrange the cooked potatoes, asparagus and cherry tomatoes around the outer edge of the leaves. Cut each loin into 3 pieces and place in the middle of the plate. Top everything with a mound of crispy fried leeks. Drizzle some extra dressing around the plate.

4 x 175g (6oz) pieces boned loin of lamb

12 cherry tomatoes, skinned

12 medium new potatoes

12 asparagus spears

salad leaves

4 tablespoons chopped herbs, including mint, chervil, chives and fennel.

4 sprigs rosemary

2 small leeks, finely shredded

8 garlic cloves lightly crushed but still whole

Vinaigrette:

2 tablespoons each balsamic vinegar, walnut oil, virgin olive oil

1 tablespoon water

1 teaspoon grain mustard

1 teaspoon honey

salt and pepper

Chocolate tart with bananas, pistachio ice cream and fresh raspberries

Warm the cream in a pan to simmering then add the chopped chocolate, allow to melt and stir well with a wooden spoon. Cool slightly and add the beaten eggs. Stir carefully, incorporating as little air as possible. Pour the mixture in to the pastry cases. Cook at 180°C/350°F/Gas Mark 4 for approximately 10 minutes until the chocolate is set. Allow to cool. Take half the raspberries and sieve into a bowl to make a coulis. Sweeten with icing sugar to taste and toss the remaining raspberries in the couli. Slice the bananas thinly and arrange on top of the tarts in a rosette shape, overlapping the edges of the pastry. Sprinkle caster sugar over the top and caramelise with a blowtorch or under a hot grill. Serve the chocolate tarts with the raspberries and ice cream and garnish with mint.

300g (10oz) dark chocolate

300ml (10fl oz) double cream

2 eggs, beaten

6 pastry tartlet cases (these can be bought ready made or baked blind)

3 bananas

450g (1lb) raspberries

caster sugar

icing sugar

Menu Four

Asparagus with Hollandaise Sauce

Pork Fillet with fondant potatoes, a tian of Mediterranean vegetables & lemon verbena gravy

Gratin of strawberries, rhubarb and elderflowers

This menu features three classic English ingredients – asparagus, pork and strawberries. There's nothing better than fresh asparagus served simply with a glossy Hollandaise. For the main course, please take the time to hunt out real pork – not that insipid, watery excuse for pork that you so often find in the supermarkets. I use Gloucester Old Spot, a rare old-fashioned breed of pig that has a sensational flavour. I'm serving it with a fresh-tasting tian of Mediterranean vegetables and a really unusual flavour – lemon verbena in the gravy. The dessert is one of my personal favourites – a fabulous marriage of strawberries, rhubarb and elderflower under a layer of bubbling, creamy sabayon. Serve it with strawberry sorbet. Sensational.

Asparagus with Hollandaise Sauce

Blanch the asparagus in boiling water for 2-3 minutes &
refresh in ice-cold water. Cut about 8 thin discs of asparagus
off each spear to use for garnish. Place the egg yolks & wine
in a stainless steel bowl and whisk vigorously over a pan of
simmering water until doubled in volume. Slowly pour in the
melted butter in a steady trickle and continue whisking. When
thickened, take off the heat and add salt, pepper, lemon juice
and chives to taste. Keep warm. Place the asparagus in a hot
pan with the olive oil and butter and sauté for 2 minutes until
hot and flecked with golden brown, then season with salt,
pepper and a squeeze of lemon juice. To serve, garnish the edge
of the plate, in a circle, with alternate pieces of asparagus and
diced tomato, arrange the asparagus in the centre of the plate
and spoon hot hollandaise sauce over the the spears. Garnish
with chive flowers and a sprig of chervil.

16 medium-sized asparagus spears
per person, trimmed.

4 tomatoes, peeled, seeded and diced

1 tablespoon of olive oil

knob of unsalted butter

sprig of chervil

a few purple chive flowers

for the Hollandaise:

4 egg yolks

100g/4oz-unsalted butter

about 50ml white wine

freshly squeezed lemon juice

handful of chopped chives

4 x 150g (5oz) portions of pork fillet, wiped dry

knob of unsalted butter

2 tablespoons olive oil

8 sprigs of rosemary

2 sprigs of lemon verbena (substitute lemon grass or lemon zest)

2-3 unpeeled garlic cloves

For the Fondant potatoes:

4 medium potatoes

100g (4oz) butter

2 cinnamon sticks

600 ml (1pt) medium cider

For the tian:

2 courgettes

2 red peppers, diced

2 yellow peppers, diced

2 aubergine, diced

2 tomatoes, skinned and chopped

10 basil leaves, shredded

1 garlic clove, crushed

3 tablespoons virgin olive oil

Peel the potatoes and take a thin slice from each of the long sides to make two flat edges. Place a flat edge down and cut a cylinder shape from each potato, with a 5cm (2in) pastry cutter. Melt the butter in a flameproof shallow dish which will take the potatoes in one layer. Add the cinnamon sticks, potatoes and salt and pepper. Pour over the cider to barely cover, then cover with foil and cook slowly on top of the s tove over a very low heat for 30 minutes or until tender. The potato will absorb all the butter, cider and flavourings and become translucent.

Slice the courgettes thinly and blanch in simmering water for 1 minute, refresh in iced water and dry. Heat the olive oil in a large pan then cook the peppers, aubergine, tomatoes and garlic for 10 minutes until softened. Stir in the basil leaves and season. Allow to cool slightly. Line the base of four microwaveable moulds (similar in diameter to the cutter used for the potatoes) with a layer of courgette slices then pack in the vegetables, pressing down well with the back of a spoon. Arrange the remaining courgettes slices on top in a rosette pattern. Leave to firm up.

Heat the butter and olive oil in a roasting tin on the hob until foaming and sear the pork fillets on a high heat for 2-3 minutes. Put a 'trivet' of the rosemary, lemon verbena and unpeeled garlic cloves under the meat to add flavour and help keep it moist. Cook at 200°C/400°F/Gas Mark 6 for 12 minutes.

Pork Fillet with fondant potatoes, a tian of Mediterranean vegetables & lemon verbena gravy

Fry any pork trimmings in the oil and butter until golden brown. Stir in the flour, cook for a minute to remove the raw flavour, and then add the cider and chicken stock. Bring to the boil, reduce in volume to about a quarter and strain. Finely chop the fresh lemon verbena sprigs and add these with the apple puree to the gravy and heat gently.

Remove the meat from the oven and rest in a warm place for 3 minutes, meanwhile heat the tians on a plate in the microwave for 1-3 minutes, depending on the power rating.

To serve, slice the pork, place a prune on each fondant potato and serve the tian of Mediterranean vegetables alongside. Spoon over the hot gravy.

For the gravy:

pork trimmings

2 tablespoons olive oil

2 tablespoons butter

2 tablespoons flour

100 ml (3fl oz) medium or dry cider

600ml (1pt) chicken stock

1tablespoon apple puree

4 prunes soaked in
2 tablespoons armagnac

2 sprigs of lemon verbena

Gratin of strawberries, rhubarb & elderflowers

Place 140g (5oz) of the sugar in a deep pan and cover with about 200ml (7fl oz) of water. Bring slowly to the boil to dissolve the sugar, and then lower the heat. Add the rhubarb, lemon juice and seeds from one vanilla pod and bring back to a simmer. Poach for about six minutes until tender. Transfer the rhubarb to a bowl and add the halved strawberries. Put the elderflowers into the rhubarb juice in the pan and infuse over a gentle heat for 10 minutes, making sure the mixture doesn't boil.

To make the sabayon, whisk the egg yolks and remaining sugar in a bowl over simmering water until thick and creamy. Strain 75ml (2fl oz) of the rhubarb syrup into the eggs and whisk for 2–3 minutes to increase the volume. In a separate bowl, whisk the whipped cream with the seeds from the remaining vanilla pod, then fold into the egg mixture. Mix gently with the fruit and divide between 4 shallow, heatproof dishes (at this point the gratin can be chilled for several hours). When ready to eat, place under a hot grill until golden brown and bubbling – about 4 minutes. Serve with ice cream or strawberry sorbet, which is sensational.

20 strawberries, hulled and halved

3 sticks of rhubarb, cut into 3cm (1in) pieces

3 heads of elderflowers

2 vanilla pods

100ml (3fl oz) whipping cream

3 egg yolks

Juice of 2 lemons

200g (7oz) caster sugar

Ice cream or strawberry sorbet to serve

Menu Five

**Pike sausage with a
watercress broth**

**Pheasant Pithivier with
root vegetables**

**Walnut and Stilton
savoury with a port and
Stilton glaze**

The pike for this dish was wrestled manfully from Fort Henry Lake on Lord Gainsborough's estate by my friend, Barry Thompson, on a fly. And on camera. No mean feat. But not wanting to leave anything to chance, Barry had a back-up plan. Stashed in the boot of his car was a 30lb monster he'd caught the previous day on Rutland Water. And before you pull a face at pike, it's a fine, tasty fish, albeit very bony. If you can't get hold of one use any good white fish such as turbot, lemon sole or Dover Sole. A pithivier is traditionally a French dessert – a puff pastry case containing almond paste. Here, I've adapted it to capture the flavours of the English game season. It's also great for a dinner party as it looks impressive and it can be prepared two days ahead. Keeping actually improves the flavour.

Pike Sausage with a watercress broth

Blend the fish and egg yolk in a food processor until smooth. Add 150ml (5fl oz) of the cream, then strain into a bowl and chill for 30 minutes. Slowly beat in the remaining cream, season with salt, pepper and a pinch of cayenne and chill for a further 30 minutes. Spoon a quarter of the mixture into the middle of a piece of cling film, fold the film over and roll into a cylinder. Pinch both ends together and squeeze the mixture into the centre to make a sausage shape. Tie the ends with string. Sweat the shallots and garlic in a little olive oil and butter until transparent. Add the potato and wine and boil for 5 minutes. Add the stock and boil for 5 minutes, then add the cream and chopped chervil and boil for a further 5 minutes. Leave to go cold. Blanch the watercress in boiling salted water for 30 seconds and then immediately add to the cooled mixture and liquidise. Poach the sausages in simmering water for 5 minutes, unwrap and gently fry in a non-stick pan, in a dash of olive oil, until golden brown.

Warm the broth, season to taste and spoon onto serving dish. Place a pike sausage in the centre and serve.

400g (14oz) skinned pike/fish fillet

1 egg yolk

350ml (12fl oz) double cream

pinch cayenne pepper

salt and pepper

75g (3oz) bunch of watercress, stalks removed & washed

1 medium potato, diced

Butter

2 teaspoons olive oil

300ml (10fl oz) strong chicken stock

2 shallots, chopped

1 clove garlic, crushed

75ml (2fl oz) white wine

Handful chopped chervil

Pheasant Pithivier with Root Vegetables

Soak the raisins in the balsamic vinegar for at least 1 hr.
Fry the shallots, walnuts, bacon, soaked raisins and tarragon for
2 minutes in the olive oil and butter. Leave to cool. Take 4
pheasant breast halves and chop coarsely in a blender for 10
seconds. Stir into the bacon and shallot mixture and season
with salt and pepper. For each serving place lightly oiled cling
film inside a small domed mould, cup or small pudding basin
and firmly press 2 tablespoons of the mixture into and up the
sides of the mould. Place a remaining pheasant breast portion
in the centre, and then cover with more of the stuffing mixture.
Firm down, wrap the cling film around and turn out. Re-line
each mould with film and line with puff pastry, allowing the
excess to come over the rim. Remove the film from the
pheasant domes and place inside the pastry. Cover the top with
pastry, chill for 30 minutes and turn out on to a baking sheet.
To decorate, hold the pithivier in the palm of your hand and,
starting almost at the top of the dome, make curving incisions
through the pastry, almost to the base, turning the pastry case
after each cut until it is scored all the way around. The
pithiviers will keep uncooked in the fridge for 2 days and the
flavours will improve. Brush with beaten egg and cook for
20-25 minutes at 200°C/400°F/Gas Mark 6 until golden. Serve
on a mound of cabbage stir-fried with walnuts and decorate
the plate with baby carrots, turnips and roasted shallots.
A good accompaniment to this dish is pheasant gravy, which
can be made using the remaining parts of the pheasant. Chop
the legs, bones and trimmings and fry with garlic and thyme
until golden. Sprinkle over the flour and cook for 1 minute,
then add the red wine. Boil briefly, and then add the stock.
Bring to boil, simmer and reduce until it thickens, then strain.

**4 pheasant breasts,
halved across the middle**

100g (4oz) chopped walnuts

**50g (2oz) raisins,
soaked in balsamic vinegar**

150g (5oz) smoked bacon lardons

5 shallots, chopped

15g (0.5oz) tarragon, chopped

**300g (11oz) puff pastry,
rolled out to 3mm thickness**

1 beaten egg

For the gravy:

Pheasant trimmings

I garlic clove, crushed

4 fresh thyme sprigs

2 teaspoons flour

100ml (3fl oz) red wine

**500ml (17fl oz) quality chicken
or pheasant stock**

To serve:

**Stir-fried cabbage and walnuts and
roasted baby carrots, turnips and shallots.**

Walnut and Stilton savoury with a port and Stilton glaze

First make the pastry cases by rolling out the puff pastry thinly. Cut out 12 circles of roughly 6cm (2.5in) in diameter, brush them all with beaten egg and place three circles on top of one another to make each case. Place on an oiled baking tray. To make sure they rise evenly stack metal pastry cases or moulds 8cm (3in) high at either side of the baking tray and rest another baking tray on top. This will prevent the pastry from rising too much and flipping over. Bake at 200°C/400°F/ Gas Mark 6 for 6 minutes. Then cool.

Place the Stilton and port for the glaze in a liquidiser; add the cream, egg yolks, salt and pepper and blend. This should still have chunky pieces of Stilton in it. When the pastry cases are cool, slice off the tops and put them to one side, then scoop out the pastry insides and discard; leaving a pastry pocket and a lid for each serving. Fill each case with crumbled Stilton and arrange slices of apple on top. Place each case in the centre of a plate and arrange the celery, grapes and walnuts around. Pour over the port and Stilton glaze and place under a hot grill until the glaze starts to bubble and brown. Place the lids back on each of the pastry cases and serve.

200g (7oz) puff pastry

1 egg, beaten

Stilton – about 75gm (3oz) per person

4 celery sticks cut in batons

40 grapes, halved and de–seeded

16 walnuts

1 apple, quartered and sliced thinly

for the glaze:

100g (4oz) Stilton

100ml (3fl oz) port

2 egg yolks

100ml (3fl oz) whipping cream

salt and pepper

Menu Six

Tagliatelle of freshwater crayfish

Wild duck with plum sauce, onion marmalade and parisienne of root vegetables

Fruits en papillote

Barry Thompson and I caught a basket of freshwater crayfish near Hambleton for this fricassee. Before any conservationist jumps down my throat, they were the American invaders that are making life so difficult for our English variety – so I was doing my bit for the countryside. Crayfish are delicious but a little hard to get, so you can use langoustine tails or raw tiger prawns instead. They all vary in size so use enough to satisfy your own appetite. Barry also had a hand in the main course – I went shooting with him and Tim Hart for wild ducks and after embarrassing myself by leaving the safety catch on, I eventually bagged one. This is how I cooked it. Barry supplied the small, wild plums for the sauce but any sweet red plum will do. I'm glad to say the dessert didn't have Barry's fingers in it at all.

Tagliatelle of freshwater crayfish

Sweat the garlic and shallots in the butter and oil until soft but not coloured. Add the mushrooms cut into large pieces and continue cooking until they begin to soften. Pour in the chicken stock and cream, stir and simmer for 2 minutes. Then add the crayfish, langoustine tails or tiger prawns. Crayfish are tiny so only need poaching for about 30 seconds; the other choices will need perhaps 2 minutes according to size. Don't overcook the fish. Finish the sauce by stirring in a knob of butter, the tomato dice, beans, peas, chervil and tarragon. Warm gently; add a squeeze of lemon juice then taste and season with salt and pepper.

Blanch the shredded leeks for two minutes, drain and sauté with 1 tablespoon of butter until coated. Cook the fresh tagliatelle and stir in the leek mixture. Roll the pasta around a fork and place in the centre of a deep plate. Pour the fricassee around and garnish with a sprig of fennel.

8-10 crayfish per person, shelled

450g (1lb) chanterelle mushrooms

2 shallots, finely chopped

small clove garlic, crushed

100ml (3fl oz) chicken stock

1 tablespoon whipping cream

1 tablespoon butter

1 tablespoon olive oil

lemon juice

4 tomatoes, skinned, de-seeded and diced

2 tablespoons cooked broad beans

2 tablespoons cooked peas

1 tablespoons chervil, chopped

1 teaspoon tarragon, chopped

knob of butter

lemon juice

2 leeks, shredded

75-100g (3-4oz) fresh tagliatelle per person

1 tablespoon butter

4 sprigs of fennel

2 wild duck

2 tablespoons olive oil

For the glaze:

4 tablespoons soy sauce

4 tablespoons balsamic vinegar

150g (6oz) honey

2 star anise

2 sticks of lemon grass

1in cube of fresh ginger, sliced

1 teaspoon Chinese 5-spice

1 tablespoon of butter

For the marmalade:

3 Spanish onions, thinly sliced

300ml (10fl oz) orange juice

zest of 2 oranges

1 tablespoon butter

1 tablespoon olive oil

1 tablespoon sugar

This is the second duck recipe featured in the book but while the honey roast spiced duck on page 46 is perfectly good with farmyard birds, this recipe will be so much better with a wild duck, if you can get your hands on one. As the duck has been flying around and doing all the things that ducks do in the wild, it is lean, the flesh is darker and it has a more intense flavour. You must take care not to overcook wild duck, as it hasn't anything like the protective layer of fat of its more sedentary cousin.

It is special; treat it with a bit of respect. The fresh plum sauce and almost candied onion marmalade – both of which can be made in advance – go particularly well with duck and the whole thing sits on a crisp potato galette (see page 34).

Glazed wild duck with plum sauce, onion marmalade and Parisienne of root vegetables

Prepare the vegetables by cutting into balls with a Parisienne scoop. Cook in water or chicken stock until tender. Cook the beetroot separately or it will colour the other vegetables. Toss the cooked vegetables in a little water and butter. These can be reheated for a few moments when you are ready to serve.

Sweat the onions in the butter and olive oil over a very low heat for 15 minutes until soft and just beginning to colour. Add the sugar and orange juice and cook for a further 15 minutes until caramelised and almost candied. Season with salt and pepper. This can be cooked several days ahead and reheated.

Stone the plums and add all the other ingredients, except the chicken stock, Cook gently for about 5 minutes until the plums are reduced to a pulp. Remove the spices, add the chicken stock, then liquidise and sieve. Reduce a little until you have a smooth, velvety sauce.

Sear the ducks for 5-6 minutes in oil until golden brown then cook at 200C/400F/Gas 6 for 15-20 minutes until cooked to your liking. Boil the glaze ingredients together until syrupy. Remove the duck from the oven, pour over the glaze and baste frequently while the duck rests in a warm place for 4 minutes.

To serve, arrange the Parisienne in a perfect circle around the edge of the plate. Place the potato galette in the centre, top with a spoonful of marmalade, some sliced duck breast and finally a duck leg. Spoon the sauce in the border between the galette and the vegetables.

For the Parisienne:

1 swede

1 turnip

2 carrots

2 beetroots

2 courgettes

For the sauce:

450g (1lb) ripe, red plums

the juice of 2 lemons

2 star anise

2 tablespoons honey

2 tablespoons balsamic vinegar

2 tablespoons sugar

1 cinnamon stick

1 tablespoon olive oil

1 tablespoon butter

300ml (10fl oz) chicken stock

You can use almost any fruit for this fresh and aromatic dessert – perfect to follow duck – but I would always include mango, pineapple, rhubarb, pears, plums and berries. Figs and red currants are also good. The fruits are steamed with aromatics in a tight little parcel that can be cut open at the table. Pigs' Ears are little sweet biscuits that go well with the fruit and look just like – you've guessed it – pigs' ears.

Fruits en papillote with Pigs' Ears

First make a simple syrup by melting the sugar in the water. Boil for 2 minutes then add the sieved raspberries and liqueur and heat through. Spread out a sheet of foil for each portion and cover with a sheet of silicone paper. Brush with melted butter and pile your selection of fruits, all cut to a similar size, in the centre. Top with the citrus zest, a cinnamon stick, star anise, a piece of vanilla pod, cloves and a sprig of lemon verbena. Pour a ladleful of syrup over the fruit, add a squeeze of lemon and a sprinkling of sugar and seal the parcels carefully. Place in a shallow roasting tin, with a splash of water in the bottom and cook at 200°/400°F/Gas Mark 6 for 7 minutes.

To make the Pigs' Ears, roll out the pastry as thinly as possible, brush with melted butter and dust with a little icing sugar. Roll the pastry up like a Swiss roll and cut into 2cm (half an inch) slices. Place the slices on a surface dusted with icing sugar and sprinkle more icing sugar on top. Take a rolling pin and roll the discs out thinly. Cook at 180°/350°F/Gas Mark 4 for about 5 minutes until golden brown. Let everyone cut open his or her own papillotes and serve with the Pigs' Ears and ice cream or cream.

Mixed fresh fruit

The zest of a lemon, lime and orange

4 sprigs of lemon verbena

4 sticks of cinnamon

8 cloves

4 star anise

2 vanilla pods, split

the juice of a lemon

a little sugar to taste

150ml (5fl oz) water

150ml (5fl oz) sugar

100g (4oz) raspberries, liquidised and sieved

2 tablespoons framboise (raspberry liqueur)

4 sheets of foil, 50cm sq (20in)

4 sheets of silicone paper, cut 3cm (1in) smaller than the foil

Melted butter

A sheet of readymade puff pastry

Melted butter

Icing sugar

Acknowledgements:
As much as it hurts me to do this, I must thank my kitchen brigade,
who take both the good moods and the bad moods in the right spirit,
specially Julian Carter and Simon Hadley, who has now moved on.
A huge thank you to my producer, John Dickinson, who approached me to
do the television series and to Wendy Dickinson, without whom the book
wouldn't have been possible. Gary Moyes and Stuart Woods did a great job
with the photography and Geoff Mayor, Louise Smith and Celia Berry at
Carlton Television's Picture Unit were invaluable, as were Richard and
Angela Foulds, who cast their eagle eyes and red pen over the copy.
Of course, my thanks for their support at all times, go to
my brother, Andrew and to Tim Hart.